ZAIRE

...in Pictures

Photo by Royal Museum of Central Africa

Visual Geography Series®

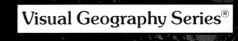

ZAIRE

...in Pictures

Prepared by
Geography Department

Lerner Publications Company
Minneapolis

Courtesy of Congopresse

**Found throughout Zaire, brightly plumed kingfishers dive
quickly to snatch their prey from ponds, marshes, and
shallow watercourses.**

This book is a newly commissioned title in the Visual
Geography Series. The text is set in 10/12 Century
Textbook.

LIBRARY OF CONGRESS CATALOGING-IN-PUBLICATION DATA

Zaire in pictures / prepared by Geography Department,
  Lerner Publications Company.
    p. cm. — (Visual geography series)
  Includes index.
  Summary: Describes the topography, history, society,
economy, and governmental structure of Zaire.
  ISBN 0-8225-1899-6 (lib. bdg.)
  1. Zaire. [1. Zaire.] I. Lerner Publications Company.
Geography Dept. II. Series: Visual geography series
(Minneapolis, Minn.)
DT644.Z345   1992
967.51—dc20   91-31006
                                                             CIP
                                                              AC

International Standard Book Number: 0-8225-1899-6
Library of Congress Catalog Card Number: 91-31006

VISUAL GEOGRAPHY SERIES®

Publisher
Harry Jonas Lerner
Senior Editor
Mary M. Rodgers
Editors
Gretchen Bratvold
Tom Streissguth
Photo Researcher
Bill Kauffmann
Editorial/Photo Assistants
Marybeth Campbell
Colleen Sexton
Consultants/Contributors
Thomas O'Toole
Phyllis Schuster
Sandra K. Davis
Designer
Jim Simondet
Cartographer
Carol F. Barrett
Indexers
Kristine S. Schubert
Sylvia Timian
Production Manager
Gary J. Hansen

Courtesy of FAO

**Zairean workers employed in a reforestation project gather
tree seedlings for replanting.**

Acknowledgments

Title page photo courtesy of Debra L. Henke.

Elevation contours adapted from *The Times Atlas of
the World,* seventh comprehensive edition (New York:
Times Books, 1985).

1 2 3 4 5 6 7 8 9 10 01 00 99 98 97 96 95 94 93 92

At Inga in western Zaire, young Zaireans get together after a church service. About half of the nation's population is under the age of 15.

Contents

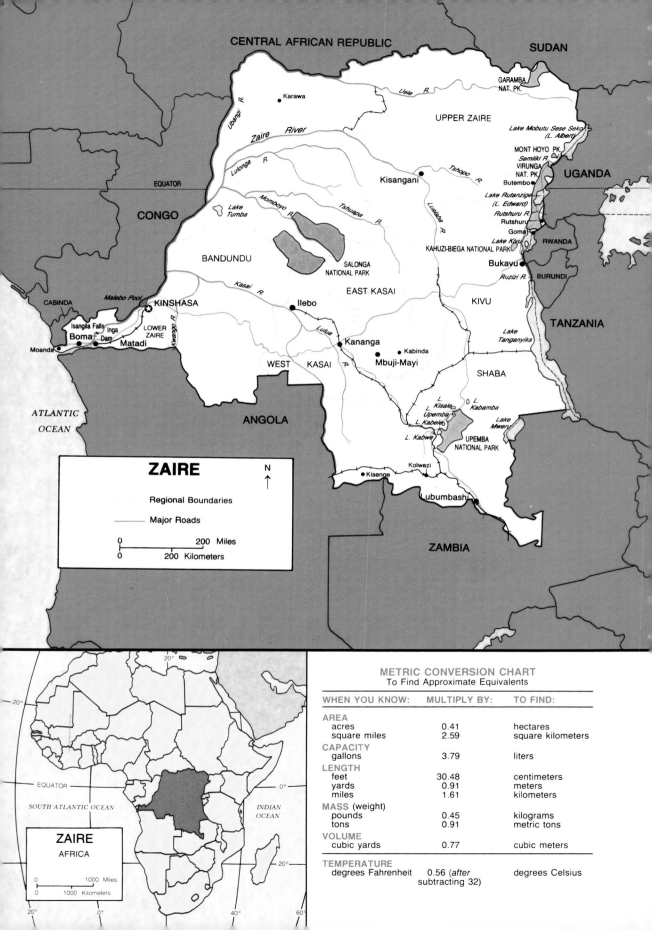

ZAIRE

N ↑

Regional Boundaries

—— Major Roads

0 ———— 200 Miles
0 ———— 200 Kilometers

CENTRAL AFRICAN REPUBLIC

SUDAN

GARAMBA NAT. PK.

UPPER ZAIRE

Karawa

Ubangi R.

Zaire River

Lulonga R.

EQUATOR

CONGO

Lake Tumba

Momboyo R.

BANDUNDU

Tshuapa R.

Kisangani

Tshopo R.

Lualaba R.

Lake Mobutu Sese Seko (L. Albert)

MONT HOYO PK
Semliki R.
VIRUNGA NAT. PK.
Butembo

UGANDA

Lake Rutanzige (L. Edward)
Rutshuru R.
Rutshuru
Goma

RWANDA

SALONGA NATIONAL PARK

KAHUZI-BIEGA NATIONAL PARK

Bukavu

Ruzizi R.

BURUNDI

CABINDA

Malebo Pool

KINSHASA

Kasai R.

EAST KASAI

KIVU

Lake Tanganyika

TANZANIA

Isangila Falls
Boma
Inga
Dam
Matadi
LOWER ZAIRE

Moanda

Kwango R.

Lulua R.

Ilebo

Kananga

Kabinda

Mbuji-Mayi

SHABA

WEST KASAI

Kasai R.

L. Kisale
L. Upemba
L. Kabele
L. Kabwe

L. Kabamba

Lake Mweru

UPEMBA NATIONAL PARK

ATLANTIC OCEAN

ANGOLA

Kisenge

Kolwezi

Lubumbashi

ZAMBIA

ZAIRE
AFRICA

EQUATOR

SOUTH ATLANTIC OCEAN

INDIAN OCEAN

0 ———— 1000 Miles
0 ———— 1000 Kilometers

METRIC CONVERSION CHART
To Find Approximate Equivalents

WHEN YOU KNOW:	MULTIPLY BY:	TO FIND:
AREA		
acres	0.41	hectares
square miles	2.59	square kilometers
CAPACITY		
gallons	3.79	liters
LENGTH		
feet	30.48	centimeters
yards	0.91	meters
miles	1.61	kilometers
MASS (weight)		
pounds	0.45	kilograms
tons	0.91	metric tons
VOLUME		
cubic yards	0.77	cubic meters
TEMPERATURE		
degrees Fahrenheit	0.56 (after subtracting 32)	degrees Celsius

Behind a small village rises Mount Sabinyo, an extinct volcano near Zaire's eastern border with Rwanda and Uganda.

Introduction

Located in west central Africa, Zaire is the continent's third largest country. The nation has 37.8 million citizens and more than 200 ethnic groups. Not one of these Zairean groups, most of which speak a Bantu language, makes up over 10 percent of the total population.

Although they live in a country that has great mineral wealth, most Zaireans do not have enough money to feed, clothe, and educate their families. In fact, if measured by average income per person, Zaire is one of the world's poorest nations.

Zaire's people have been grouped into a single nation for a relatively short time.

From the fifteenth to the late nineteenth centuries, many thriving kingdoms evolved in Zaire. Most of the people in these kingdoms lived in small villages and relied on farming, hunting, and fishing for survival. In the sixteenth century, slave trading with Europeans became an important economic activity for some local leaders. African brokers who captured villagers and sold them to foreign buyers also profited from the slave trade.

In the late 1800s, Zaire's vast store of minerals attracted Belgium's King Leopold II. He signed treaties with hundreds of African leaders to mine and sell Zaire's

In the late 1880s, when Zaire came under the control of the kingdom of Belgium, mining became a major economic activity. Here, conveyer belts add copper-filled rocks to huge piles of the mineral, which will later be smelted into ore.

resources. In 1885 the Congo Free State, which covered the area of modern Zaire, was established by the king as his personal property.

Leopold encouraged mining and became wealthy from the export of Zaire's minerals. But the king's methods were harsh. His mine operators forced people from the

In 1918 troops from Zaire—then a colony called the Belgian Congo—paraded with their Belgian officers. The soldiers participated in efforts to defeat Germany, which had occupied Belgium during World War I (1914–1918).

Congo Free State to labor in the mines without pay, and millions of workers starved. An international outcry against these practices caused the Belgian legislature to take over the Congo Free State—which was renamed the Belgian Congo—in 1908.

Exports from the Belgian Congo gave Belgium the income to rebuild its damaged cities and industries after the world wars of the early twentieth century. Within the colony, Belgian leaders maintained control, and the local people had little influence on the colonial government. During the 1950s—when other African colonies were demanding self-rule—activists in the Belgian Congo worked for independence, which they gained in 1960 through negotiation.

Few of Zaire's early leaders had the education or experience to govern the country well. Ethnic clashes, political disagreements, and civil war marked the first few years of nationhood. By 1965 the

Courtesy of N. Brodeur/FAO

Zairean women wait their turn at a health clinic near Kinshasa, the capital of Zaire.

Photo by Globe Photos, Inc.

Mobutu Sese Seko, ruler of Zaire since 1965, holds a star-studded baton as a symbol of his authority. In the early 1990s, opposition groups forced Mobutu to give up some of his powers.

head of the army, Mobutu Sese Seko, had taken over the country. He enacted strict measures to weaken ethnic ties and to reduce external control of the economy.

These changes ended some rivalries. But Mobutu's policies—which have included state control of industries and heavy borrowing from rich countries—have steadily worsened Zaire's financial standing. Agricultural production has declined, and corruption and mismanagement have hampered industrial growth. Frequently, foreign aid has been spent unwisely or has enriched political officials.

In the early 1990s, Zaire's future was uncertain. International groups pressed Mobutu to open up his government, but his half-hearted attempts angered many Zairean politicians. Unpaid soldiers rioted in the streets, destroying goods and property. Non-Zaireans, including teachers and health-care professionals, fled the country. Food and medical supplies became scarce.

Mobutu appeared unwilling either to address the nation's growing problems or to share political power. Although the president has much to lose, it is the Zairean people who will experience the long-term results of careless policies and corrupt leadership.

9

An aerial view shows the Lualaba River as it winds northward through eastern Zaire. Eventually, the waterway turns westward. At that point, it becomes the Zaire River and flows toward the Atlantic Ocean.

1) The Land

Zaire is the largest African nation after Sudan and Algeria. With 905,365 square miles of territory, Zaire is one-third the size of the United States. The equator runs through northern Zaire, which is landlocked except for an extremely short western coast on the Atlantic Ocean.

Zaire shares land boundaries with nine countries and one territory. Southwest of Zaire is Angola, and Zambia sits to the south and southeast. Tanzania, Burundi, Rwanda, and Uganda border Zaire to the east. Sudan and northeastern Zaire share a boundary, and the Central African Republic lies to the north. To the northwest are the Republic of the Congo and the Angolan territory of Cabinda, which is located north of Zaire's 25-mile seacoast.

Topography

Zaire's four major geographical regions show the variety of the landscapes in central Africa. The Central Zaire Basin stretches across the northern and central parts of the country. The Northern Uplands, the Southern Uplands, and the Eastern Highlands cover the remaining areas and nearly surround the basin.

The Central Zaire Basin spans one-third of the nation's territory and is cut almost in half by the equator. The region is often called the *cuvette*—which means "basin" in French, the nation's official language. Rainfall in the cuvette is very high, and a dense rain-forest dominates the region. The soil of the Central Zaire Basin is not very fertile. As a result, the region supports only a few farms and has a sparse population.

The Northern Uplands form a narrow band along the northern border of Zaire.

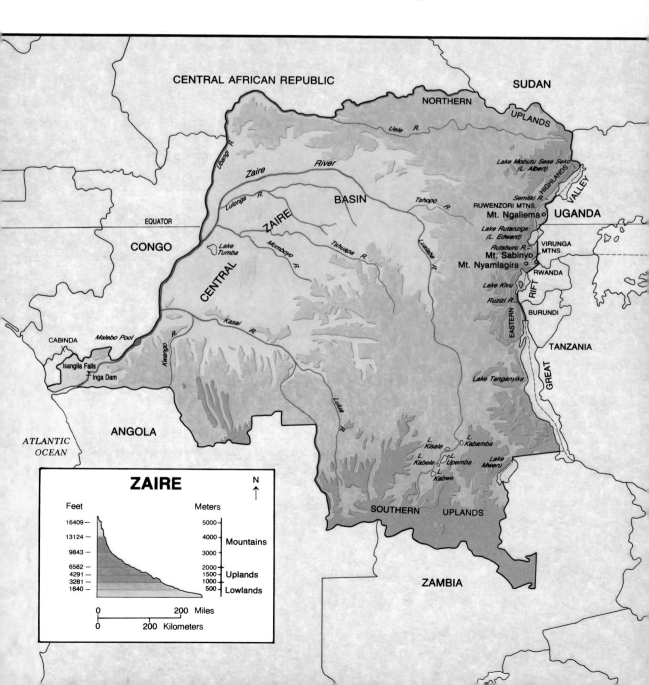

ZAIRE

Farmers who live in the small villages of the Eastern Highlands cultivate the region's fertile volcanic soil.

Savannas—grasslands with scattered trees—cover most of the region. The average elevation is 1,640 feet, but the Northern Uplands rise to heights of 2,500 feet in the northeast.

Savannas and woodlands also cover the high, flat Southern Uplands, which begin south of the Central Zaire Basin. With an average altitude of 2,730 feet above sea level, these high plains have distinct seasons and are cooler and drier than the cuvette. The climate and soil allow local people to grow grains, such as corn and millet, and to raise cattle. Within the Southern Uplands is the Shaba region, which contains many of Zaire's mineral deposits.

The Eastern Highlands extend 950 miles southward from Lake Mobutu Sese Seko (also called Lake Albert) to the southernmost edge of the Shaba region. The highlands lie along an arm of the Great Rift Valley, a long, deep trench that stretches from the Middle East to southeastern Africa. Covered with thick forests and grasslands, the Eastern Highlands have fertile farmland and are densely populated.

A rugged series of high plateaus and mountain ranges, the Eastern Highlands reach the greatest altitudes in Zaire. The region's tallest mountain group is the Ruwenzori, which crosses the equator south of Lake Mobutu Sese Seko. The highest peak in the range—snow-capped Mount Ngaliema—rises to 16,791 feet.

South of the Ruwenzori are the Virunga Mountains, which include active volcanoes. Of the eight main volcanoes in the range, Mount Nyamlagira is the most active. It spews lava, smoke, and fire every three to four years.

Rivers and Lakes

The Zaire River (also called the Congo River) and its tributaries form the country's major transportation system. The 2,900-mile-long Zaire, the longest river in Africa after the Nile, flows through the cuvette. This area receives some of the heaviest annual rainfall in the world.

The Zaire River forms gradually. Streams flowing out of the Eastern Highlands combine to make the Lualaba River, which receives the water of other rivers west of the city of Kisangani. At this point, the Lualaba is renamed the Zaire and begins to curve northwestward and then southward.

Mighty tributaries that run through the cuvette swell the volume of the Zaire. At the Zairean capital of Kinshasa, 200 miles east of the Atlantic Ocean, the river widens into the Malebo Pool, a 50-mile-long lake. After exiting the lake, the Zaire continues westward toward the sea.

About 1,860 miles of the Zaire River are navigable. High waterfalls and dangerous rapids make transportation impossible on some sections. The major navigable tributaries of the Zaire are the Kasai, Tshuapa, and Ubangi rivers. The Ubangi forms the boundary between Zaire and countries to the west and north.

Zaire's largest lakes are in the Eastern Highlands along the edge of the Great Rift Valley. These lakes serve as recreational areas and as major transportation routes between Zaire and eastern Africa. Less busy are Shaba's plateau lakes, which are the remains of an inland sea that covered Zaire millions of years ago. Teeming with fish, these bodies of water include Lakes Kisale, Kabwe, Kabele, Kabamba, and Upemba.

Lake Tanganyika—a 415-mile-long body of water between Zaire and Tanzania—is the world's second deepest lake after Lake Baikal in Russia. The Ruzizi River

Rapids hamper navigation on the Zaire River. This rough section begins west of Kinshasa.

The winding course of the Rutshuru River makes hairpin turns in northeastern Zaire before reaching Lake Rutanzige (also called Lake Edward).

connects Lake Tanganyika to Lake Kivu, which is 62 miles long. Farther north, the Semliki River links Lake Rutanzige (also called Lake Edward) and Lake Mobutu Sese Seko. Streams that flow out of both lakes contribute to the headwaters (source) of the Nile River.

Climate

A huge country, Zaire experiences a wide variety of climates. North of the equator, a dry season occurs from about early November to late March. That same period is the rainy season in sections of the country south of the equator. Local topographical features affect this general pattern, however, and some places have two wet seasons and two dry seasons per year.

Yearly rainfall varies from 40 to 80 inches or more in Zaire. The heaviest amount falls in the west and in the cuvette, where downpours happen almost every day of the rainy season. Parts of southern Shaba, on the other hand, experience occasional droughts.

Temperatures and humidity remain quite high throughout most of Zaire. The hottest weather occurs in the equatorial forest, where daytime readings average about 90° F and nighttime temperatures rarely fall below 70° F. Seasonal variations exist in the Southern Uplands, particularly in southeastern Shaba, where cool, dry winters and warm, wet summers are the rule. Shaba's average daytime temperature is about 75° F.

A mild, moist climate prevails in the Eastern Highlands. The average reading is 64° F, and seasonal temperature variations in the region are slight. Humidity is high in the mountains and increases with elevation. Mists hide many of the tall slopes throughout the year.

Courtesy of National Museum of African Art, Eliot Elisofon Archives, Smithsonian Institution

Heavy rains stranded this truck in northern Zaire. The country's 80 inches of annual precipitation have a disastrous effect on the nation's road network.

Flora and Fauna

Eight reserves, which together cover 15 percent of the nation's territory, help to protect Zaire's abundant wildlife and plants. Some of the country's animal species, however, are threatened with extinction. For example, poachers (people who hunt illegally) have nearly wiped out Zaire's elephant population. They kill these animals for their ivory tusks, which are exported to make ivory statues, jewelry, or handicrafts.

Virunga National Park, the biggest reserve, is home to buffalo, antelope, lions, leopards, elephants, monkeys, baboons, jackals, and hyenas. Many of Zaire's bird species—such as sunbirds, weavers, honey guides, partridges, storks, eagles, and cranes—also inhabit the park. Thousands of hippopotamuses roam the vast grasslands near the Rutshuru River in eastern Zaire. The Mont Hoyo reserve in eastern Zaire shelters chimpanzees and many other kinds of apes, including the unusual black-and-white colobus.

Kahuzi-Biega National Park near Bukavu is the home of the endangered mountain gorilla. Garamba National Park, which borders Sudan, is the last refuge of the white (square-lipped) rhinoceros, another animal threatened with extinction. Upemba park contains zebras, eland, black antelope, and other hoofed animals. The okapi —which looks like a mix of a horse, a zebra, and a donkey—lives only in northeastern Zaire. Scientists continue to study the thousands of species in the Salonga reserve, a huge park in Zaire's rain-forest.

Zaire's vegetation is as varied as its wildlife. Palm trees and aloe plants grow throughout the country. Trees that yield copal resin—which can be made into lubricants or plastics—frequently reach more than 100 feet in height and are often covered with vines. Mangrove trees spread their huge, clawlike roots in marshy areas and along riverbanks.

The dense rain-forest that covers a large part of Zaire is one of the least explored

Photo by John Edward Hayashida

Elephants wander amid the scrub vegetation of Virunga National Park, which lies near Lake Rutanzige in eastern Zaire.

Courtesy of J. J. Leroy/FAO

This male mountain gorilla lives in Kahuzi-Biega National Park. Shy and protective of family members, mountain gorillas have been illegally hunted nearly to extinction. Only about 350 of the animals still exist.

15

Water hyacinths flourish in Zaire's tropical regions, sometimes crowding fish and other creatures out of their habitats.

areas on earth. Even local hunters rarely venture beyond the forest clearings. At least 10,000 kinds of flowering plants grow in Zaire's rain-forest. A wide variety of hardwood trees—such as the wenge, the iroko, the black mubangu, the tola, and the limba—also thrive. Loggers harvest some of the trees for export.

Trees of the Eastern Highlands include eucalyptus and pine, both of which were brought to the region by Europeans. Dense bamboo forests grow at elevations above 6,800 feet. Higher still are lobelias, briers, lichens, and orchids. These plants can survive cooler conditions. In southern Shaba are baobab trees, whose thick bark protects them from drying out during the area's long rainless season.

The plants commonly known as elephants' ears thrive in the shade of tropical trees. The leaves of these plants can grow to be about two feet wide.

The Rutshuru River is home to these hippos, who eat vegetation growing both in the river and on its banks.

Photo by Daniel H. Condit

A lion in Virunga National Park appears in the golden light of early morning.

Photo by John Edward Hayashida

Courtesy of John Vreyens

Among the most abundant animals in the rain-forests are insects, such as this large butterfly that temporarily rests on a large tropical leaf.

Natural Resources

Zaire has a wealth of natural resources. Large copper deposits exist in the Shaba region, which also has reserves of cobalt, cadmium, uranium, tin, silver, and gold. The Zairean government grants leases to Belgian, Japanese, and U.S. companies to mine oil fields that are located in the country's small section of the Atlantic Ocean.

The regions of West Kasai and East Kasai in south central Zaire have considerable supplies of diamonds. Workers shape the diamonds into cutting tools that can be used in high-technology industries. In addition, Zaire's powerful rivers possess valuable hydroelectrical potential. Engineers have built dams and other hydropower structures in the Lower Zaire region near the Atlantic coast.

Cities

About 40 percent of Zaire's nearly 38 million citizens live in urban areas. The percentage is growing as young villagers leave rural areas for towns and cities in search of jobs. Many government officials and leading businesspeople have comfortable, modern urban homes. Most factory and office workers, however, endure crowded conditions in poorly constructed houses and apartments.

KINSHASA

With about four million residents in its metropolitan area, Kinshasa—the capital of Zaire—is the country's largest urban center. Formerly named Leopoldville, the city sits on the Zaire River about 200 miles inland from the Atlantic Ocean. The site was a small village in 1880, when the British

An open-pit copper mine in the Shaba region of southern Zaire reveals many layers of digging. For decades, these mines have yielded vast amounts of the metal, which has provided a large income to the national government.

Completed in the 1970s, the Inga Dam on the Zaire River produces electricity for industries in the southern part of the country.

In 1991 riots erupted in Kinshasa as soldiers protested long-overdue wages by looting and burning businesses.

June 30 Boulevard—named after the date of national independence from colonial rule—nearly spans the width of Kinshasa. Eight lanes accommodate heavy traffic, and shops, office buildings, and government agencies face the street.

explorer Henry Stanley obtained a treaty for Belgium's King Leopold II to govern the area. The king made the village the capital of the Congo Free State.

With one-third of Zaire's industries and with good transportation links, Kinshasa is also the country's main economic center. The capital's manufacturing plants produce textiles, clothing, footwear, tires, and chemicals. Other industries include shipbuilding, steelmaking, sawmills, palm-oil processing, and motor-vehicle assembly. Kinshasa has a campus of the National University of Zaire, as well as several other schools of higher education.

SECONDARY CITIES

Lubumbashi (population 800,000) sits on a high plateau north of the Kasai River, which separates Zaire from Zambia. Formerly called Elisabethville, Lubumbashi is both the capital of Shaba, the nation's copper-mining center, and Zaire's second largest urban area.

Open-pit and underground mines dominate Lubumbashi. The city also has factories that process copper and that refine the by-products of copper ore. Large piles of waste from these activities are visible from miles away, and factory chimneys that spew thick smoke mark the skyline. Lubumbashi's other industrial products include cigarettes, textiles, shoes, palm oil, and processed foods.

Named for a leader of the Lulua people, Kananga (population 490,000) is the capital of West Kasai. Situated on the Lulua River, the city is an administrative, transportation, and milling center. In 1970, however, Kananga lost its position as the hub of Zaire's diamond-marketing industry to Mbuji-Mayi, the capital of East Kasai. Since then, many of Kananga's roads and industries have declined.

Kisangani (population 350,000)—formerly called Stanleyville—is the capital of the Upper Zaire region, which covers the northeastern part of the country. The city sits at the junction of the Zaire and Tshopo rivers but is separated from the navigable portion of the Zaire by 125 miles of rapids and waterfalls. Railways and roads link the city to other parts of northeastern Zaire. Kisangani also has a campus of the National University of Zaire.

Once a fishing village and trading post, Kisangani became a major port for trade in farming and mining goods in the late 1800s. In the 1960s, violence during the Zairean civil war rocked the city, killing many people and damaging houses, businesses, and the local economy. Fishing is still an important industry near Kisangani. In recent years, the government has attempted to revive agriculture and manufacturing in the area.

Located in southern Zaire, Lubumbashi is the region's industrial hub and has the best rail connections to other parts of the country.

Musicians accompany the king of Kongo on a stroll in this European drawing from the 1500s. The Kongo kingdom was the first of several powerful realms that developed in Zaire.

2) History and Government

Historians believe ancestors of the Mbuti were the earliest inhabitants of Zaire. They may have settled in the dense rain-forest as long as 10,000 years ago, establishing stable hunting and gathering communities. Many of the Mbuti who live in the Central Zaire Basin still follow this lifestyle in modern times.

Further archaeological evidence suggests that groups of people who spoke Bantu languages began to move into Zaire from western Africa after about 1000 B.C. The Bantu-speakers were farmers and herders as well as hunters and gatherers. Over the course of many centuries, these peoples spread throughout the Central Zaire Basin in search of food.

Many Bantu-speakers settled south of Zaire's rain-forest in the grasslands and eventually learned to make iron tools. They also fashioned copper into jewelry and into ingots (solid bars) that could be used as money. As Bantu-speaking groups migrated farther southward and northward across the rain-forest, they spread the knowledge of metalworking throughout the region.

By about A.D. 800, Zaire contained a mixture of Bantu-speaking peoples from western, north central, and east central Africa. Over time, but probably from the twelfth century onward, some of these groups began to organize into small, wealthy communities led by nobles. West of Lake Tanganyika, archaeologists have discovered graves of these leaders that contain copper, iron, and ivory jewelry. Bracelets, bells, and other metal goods have also been found in tombs in the Shaba region.

Kingdoms Arise

In about 1400, ethnic groups from northern Africa began to migrate into northern Zaire. They intermarried with the Bantu-speaking peoples, and a new mosaic of cultures emerged. At about the same time, the Bantu-speaking communities of western and southern Zaire were combining into large kingdoms.

The largest of the Zairean kingdoms were the Kongo, the Luba, the Lunda, and the Kuba. In each realm, the lines of authority were strict, with local leaders (or chiefs) owing loyalty and goods to more powerful regional rulers. This system reached upward to the king, who was usually elected from among the male members of an elite group.

Two other sizable Bantu-speaking kingdoms—the Teke and the Chokwe—also developed in Zaire at this time. The Teke settled on both sides of the Zaire River in the northwest. The Chokwe lived near the upper Kwango and Kasai rivers in southwestern Zaire.

KONGO AND LUBA

Kongo was centered north of the mouth of the Zaire River. In the 1400s, this realm

invaded lands south of the river. Eventually, in addition to Zaire, Kongo covered parts of what are now Angola and the Republic of the Congo. Peoples subdued by the Kongo kingdom were accepted into the population rather than ruled as conquered subjects. Local leaders exercised religious as well as political power. The importance of local rulers eventually lessened the authority of Kongo's central government.

In the mid-1400s, after the Kongo kingdom was enlarged, villages in the grasslands south of the Central Zaire Basin began to combine into small states. Traditional stories say that an outside group of Bantu-speakers, called the Lopwe, sped up the process by organizing the villages into a single political unit. Under the skilled leadership of Lopwe kings, the Luba kingdom emerged. The Luba realm, which was

Courtesy of National Museum of Denmark, Ethnography Department

For the ancient peoples of Zaire, carved wooden masks represented local leaders or vital life forces that influenced daily events. The masks were part of fertility rites and funerals. This example comes from the Chokwe people, who lived in southwestern Zaire.

centered between the Kasai River and Lake Tanganyika, had a strong government that was dominated by the Lopwe nobility.

LUNDA AND KUBA

A new realm, the Lunda kingdom, formed in the 1500s from a split in the Luba nobility. The brother of a Luba king moved southwestward and founded the Lunda realm, which straddled the boundary of present-day Angola and Zaire. After conquering the local leaders, the Lunda king let the former chiefs retain some power in exchange for money and goods. Lunda nobles also inherited the status, name, and family of the conquered leaders.

The Kuba, who gained wealth from fishing, arrived in central Zaire from western Africa sometime during the 1500s. In later centuries, they added the cultivation of corn, cassava (a starchy root), and tobacco to their economy. The Kuba developed advanced methods of building, of making tools, and of storing food.

Portuguese Influence

While these various kingdoms were forming, European traders were beginning to

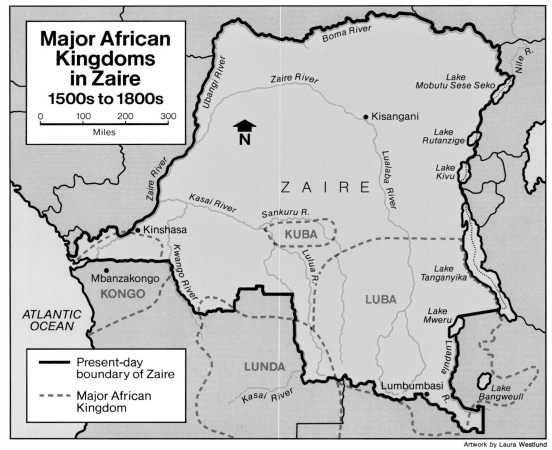

Artwork by Laura Westlund

Over a period of several centuries, large and small kingdoms evolved in Zaire. This map shows the general locations of the Kongo, the Luba, the Lunda, and the Kuba domains.

24

Brokers guide a group of captured human beings to a station in central Africa. Although the slave trade had existed in the early Zairean kingdoms, it did not become a major economic activity until Europeans arrived in the 1500s.

explore coastal areas of the African continent. One of the first Europeans to arrive on Zaire's shores was the Portuguese trader Diogo Cão, who reached the mouth of the Zaire River in 1482. He soon made contact with the Kongo kingdom at its capital of Mbanzakongo (now in Angola).

In the 1490s, the Portuguese brought Roman Catholic missionaries to Kongo with the intention of converting the king and his family to the Catholic faith. Nzinga Mbemba, who succeeded to Kongo's throne in 1507, became a Christian and took the name Afonso I.

Afonso admired the ways of the Portuguese and tried to install European practices in his realm. He signed trading contracts with Europeans, encouraged Christian missionary work, and allowed some of his subjects to be educated in Portugal.

THE SLAVE TRADE

Although the slave trade had existed for centuries in Africa, the Portuguese and other Europeans greatly expanded it. The Portuguese, for example, exported large numbers of African laborers to farming estates the Portuguese had established in Brazil, South America. In the Kongo kingdom, Portuguese merchants exchanged cloth, manufactured goods, and jewelry for ivory, copper, and slaves.

Few Europeans ventured inland to capture slaves. The Portuguese preferred to deal with African brokers, who brought captives and goods to settlements near the coast. Afonso soon recognized, however, that slave trading was rapidly depopulating his country's interior. He complained to the Portuguese king, who had no intention of ending the trade. Afonso's reluctance to allow more and more of his subjects to be taken as slaves caused the Portuguese to seek other means of acquiring them.

In the late 1500s, to maintain a constant supply of slaves, Portugal established Angola as a colony south of the Kongo kingdom. From this base, the Portuguese encouraged warlike African groups to raid the interior and to kidnap people. Despite

25

these practices, Portugal maintained peaceful ties with Kongo and continued to send missionaries to the kingdom.

Kongo's Decline and Its Aftermath

In 1568 a group of African warriors attacked Mbanzakongo in an attempt to take control of the slave trade. The Kongo king at the time—Alvaro I—called for Portugal's help. Backed by Portuguese forces, Alvaro drove out the invaders in 1573. To repay Portugal for its aid, Alvaro allowed slave trading to increase and to reach farther inland.

In spite of this agreement, economic rivalry among European nations brought increasing conflict to the African kingdoms in Zaire. In the early 1600s, the Dutch fleet was threatening Portugal's commercial power in Africa. In addition, Dutch, French, and British merchants arrived on the West African coast and began taking captives from Kongo.

Seeking even greater freedom to catch slaves, the Dutch supported Kongo factions that opposed the king. Dutch efforts to dislodge the Kongo monarch met with little success, however, and the Dutch turned their attention to Angola, which they seized from Portugal in 1641.

In 1648 the Portuguese regained Angola and from there renewed their earlier attempts to influence Kongo. Years of slave trading had weakened the Kongo kingdom. As a result, when war broke out between Angola and Kongo in 1665, the Portuguese-backed Angolan soldiers easi-

Photo by Royal Museum of Central Africa

A drawing shows the Kongo monarch Alvaro I receiving petitions from Europeans at his capital in Mbanzakongo (now in Angola).

By the 1700s, slave trading had increased so much that the Europeans were building special ports on the African coast to handle the traffic. In time, other kingdoms in Zaire took over the slave trade from Kongo. The Lunda realm, which expanded throughout the 1700s, sent its warriors to raid Luba territories for slaves and ivory. The people and goods were exchanged with the Europeans for copper and salt. The Lunda king also kept some of the captives to work on his farms.

In the 1800s, many Zairean people forced into slavery were sent eastward to Tanzania or to Zanzibar in East Africa, where the demand for slave laborers was strong. Some brokers shipped their captives as far as the Middle East. By the mid-1800s, Kiswahili-speaking merchants from eastern Africa were dominating the trade. While pursuing their interests, they often

Courtesy of Smith College of Art

An artisan from the Luba kingdom carved this ceremonial ax with the figure of a woman's head at the end of the handle.

ly defeated the Kongo army. To further disrupt the kingdom, the Portuguese purchased prisoners of war as slaves.

EFFECTS OF THE SLAVE TRADE

After the decline of Kongo in the late 1600s, the slave trade increased, with buyers from Italy, Denmark, Sweden, and later the United States taking as many as 15,000 people from Zaire each year. Slavery tore African families apart and caused political systems to break down. To escape enslavement, villages revolted against their local leaders. In turn, the leaders rebelled against the more powerful central authorities, many of whom were making money from the trade.

Photo by Bettmann/Hulton

Tippu Tib—a Kiswahili-speaking merchant—ran a successful commercial operation in the Zairean interior from the 1850s to the 1880s. His main items of trade were slaves and ivory.

27

In the 1870s, the British journalist and adventurer Henry Stanley ventured down the Zaire River. At some points, heavy rains hampered travel by boat. Here, local guides help Stanley through a turbulent section. Stanley's trek brought attention to Zaire, which Europeans knew as the Congo. Among Stanley's most enthusiastic listeners was the king of Belgium, Leopold II. He was looking for new sources of wealth and was attracted by Stanley's reports of the Congo's abundant natural resources, particularly rubber and copper.

Photo by Royal Museum of Central Africa

interfered with local Zairean politics. In time, Kiswahili became an important language in the Eastern Highlands.

One of these Kiswahili-speakers, an Arab-African trader named Tippu Tib, reached Luba in the 1850s. With a staff of about 4,000 people, he set up his own state on the Lualaba River, from which he traded slaves for many years. At about the same time, a merchant named Msiri acted as a go-between for Arab traders and Shaba leaders. Eventually, he established a commercial operation similar to Tippu Tib's that prospered from the sale of copper, ivory, and slaves. Both of these states flourished until the late 1800s, when European countries outlawed the slave trade.

Exploration and Colonization

Looking for raw materials with which to make finished goods, Europeans explored Zaire extensively throughout the 1800s. In 1816 a British group sailed up the Zaire River to Isangila Falls and brought back detailed studies of the area. Other expeditions in the mid-1800s reached Lake Tanganyika. The Scottish missionary David Livingstone spread knowledge of Zaire—called the Congo by Europeans—through newspaper accounts of a series of explorations he made from 1840 to 1872.

In 1874 a British journalist named Henry Stanley undertook a journey through what is now Zaire. Starting from East Africa, he sailed down the Zaire

River, arriving at the Atlantic Ocean on March 12, 1877. Although he failed to interest the British in further exploration, his trip attracted the attention of King Leopold II of Belgium.

Leopold's ambitions for territory and riches far exceeded the resources of the small European kingdom of Belgium. In Stanley's reports, Leopold saw an opportunity to make money from the sale of Zaire's natural resources, including rubber, ivory, and copper. Leopold hired Stanley to explore the Central Zaire Basin and to negotiate trade agreements with local leaders. In 1880 Stanley founded the village of Vivi at the mouth of the Zaire River and then moved upstream to a wide part in the river that he named Stanley Pool (now Malebo Pool). At that site, he established the settlement of Leopoldville (modern Kinshasa).

In 1884, after completing another expedition for Leopold, Stanley returned to Europe with more than 400 treaties signed by Zairean leaders. In these documents, the leaders gave Leopold the rights to much of the land and resources in Zaire in exchange for improvements in living conditions and protection from slave trading. Leopold also gained the labor of the people living in Zaire. Later that year, 13 European nations met to divide the African continent into colonies. In 1885 these nations recognized Zaire, then called the Congo Free State, as the personal property of Leopold II.

Leopold set up an administrative system to develop the region. The new government claimed for Leopold all lands that were not immediately occupied—99 percent of Zaire's territory. The king gave private European companies exclusive

Leopold II's interest in the Congo resulted in the region becoming his personal property as the Congo Free State. This cartoon shows the international reaction to Leopold's takeover. The king is depicted as a snake strangling a Congolese man as his wife and child try to escape.

Independent Picture Service

rights to collect rubber and ivory, to mine copper, and to plant cash crops on large tracts of land. In return, the companies paid the king a percentage of their profits.

The colonial administration disrupted the lives of the local people, whom the Belgians called Congolese. European officials ended the rule of local leaders and operated with little concern for ethnic groupings or traditions. Mining companies, for example, took men from their families and moved them to work sites hundreds of miles away. Despite the European ban on slavery, the men labored for no pay and received little food.

Laws established the amounts of marketable produce, such as rubber and food crops, that local workers had to give the companies. Sometimes, if the quotas were not met, Leopold's administrators destroyed entire villages. People who resisted these practices were beaten or executed. Some historians estimate that eight million workers lost their lives in the Congo Free State through these harsh practices.

The Belgian Congo

In the early 1900s, reports from missionaries and diplomats about Leopold's offenses against the Congolese caused an outcry in Europe and in the United States. International criticism of Leopold's rule became so great that on November 15, 1908, the Belgian legislature took possession of the region, making the Congo Free State a colony called the Belgian Congo. Thereafter, the Belgian nation—rather than Leopold II—received the colony's profits. Life for most Congolese workers, however, did not change.

The Belgian parliament had official authority over the Belgian Congo. But, in practice, a few powerful European companies administered the colony for Belgium and controlled most of Zaire's wealth.

As a result of the Belgian legislature's disinterest, abuses of the Congolese continued. In 1910, for example, Belgian mer-

THE GUILT OF DELAY.

By the early 1900s, reports from the Congo Free State showed that Belgian officials were abusing the local people. Over several years, debates took place in Europe on the subject of stopping Leopold's activities. As this drawing suggests, however, the delay allowed the abuses to continue.

chants proposed the building of a railway to transport goods from southern regions and from the Central Zaire Basin to port cities. Harsh working conditions caused many Congolese to die during the railway's construction. The abuses sparked labor riots, which Belgian colonial officials put down by force.

WORLD WAR I

In the 1910s, Belgium was more immediately concerned with events happening in Europe than with the affairs of the Belgian Congo. Belgium's neighbor Germany opposed France and Britain in a struggle for international territory and trading strength. Their rivalry eventually led to the outbreak of World War I (1914–1918). To strike at France, Germany invaded and occupied Belgium during the conflict.

Photo by Bettmann Archive

The Belgian government ended Leopold's personal control of the Congo Free State in 1908. Thereafter, the government received the profits of diamond mining *(above)*. To better transport goods to the Congo's ports, the Belgians organized the construction of a railroad *(below)*.

Photo by Royal Museum of Central Africa

European Powers in Africa

(Late 1800s and Early 1900s)

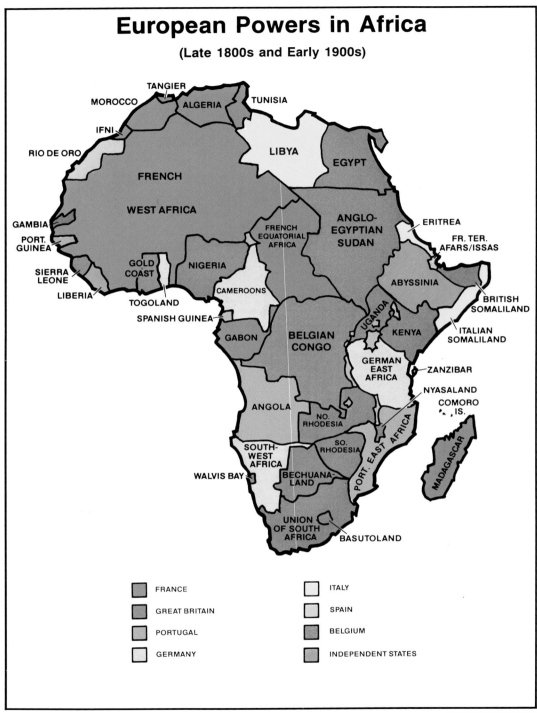

TANGIER
MOROCCO
ALGERIA
TUNISIA
IFNI
RIO DE ORO
LIBYA
EGYPT
FRENCH
WEST AFRICA
FRENCH EQUATORIAL AFRICA
ANGLO-EGYPTIAN SUDAN
ERITREA
FR. TER. AFARS/ISSAS
GAMBIA
PORT. GUINEA
SIERRA LEONE
LIBERIA
GOLD COAST
NIGERIA
CAMEROONS
TOGOLAND
SPANISH GUINEA
GABON
ABYSSINIA
BRITISH SOMALILAND
ITALIAN SOMALILAND
UGANDA
KENYA
BELGIAN CONGO
GERMAN EAST AFRICA
ZANZIBAR
NYASALAND
COMORO IS.
ANGOLA
NO. RHODESIA
SO. RHODESIA
PORT. EAST AFRICA
MADAGASCAR
SOUTH-WEST AFRICA
WALVIS BAY
BECHUANA-LAND
UNION OF SOUTH AFRICA
BASUTOLAND

FRANCE
GREAT BRITAIN
PORTUGAL
GERMANY
ITALY
SPAIN
BELGIUM
INDEPENDENT STATES

Artwork by Larry Kaushansky

The Belgian government renamed the Congo Free State the Belgian Congo. The arrival of Belgian colonial officials in Africa furthered the use of French, which Belgians speak. The spread of the Roman Catholic faith, which most Belgians follow, also resulted from colonial rule. (Colonial map information from *The Anchor Atlas of World History,* 1978.)

The Belgian Congo provided soldiers and important raw materials to the countries allied against Germany. Troops from the Belgian Congo fought German forces in the German colonies of Tanganyika (modern Tanzania) and Cameroon. Revenues from the Belgian Congo's exports helped to support the Belgian government while it was in exile during the war.

The 1920s and 1930s

After the war ended in 1918, Belgium turned its attention to its colonial activities. Like other European powers, Belgium saw itself as the caretaker for peoples not yet ready to look after themselves. Although a few of the local people disagreed with this view, they had little power or opportunity to change it.

Soldiers from the Belgian Congo fought in Tanganyika (modern Tanzania) and in Cameroon during World War I.

Photo by Royal Museum of Central Africa

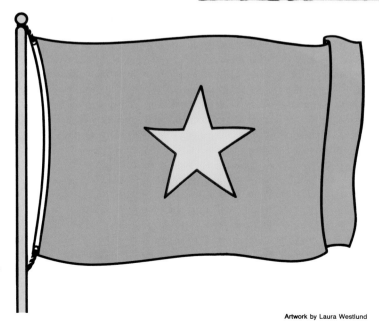

Artwork by Laura Westlund

Adopted in the late 1800s, the flag of the Belgian Congo (left) **flew next to the national flag of Belgium until independence in 1960. Blue stood for the waters of the Zaire River, and the yellow star symbolized the light of hope.**

Photo by Royal Museum of Central Africa

Roman Catholic nuns pose with their pupils outside a school set up in the Belgian Congo. The colonial government helped to support these mission schools, where job skills were taught along with religious beliefs.

A professional class of Belgian civil servants ran the colony and developed medical facilities and a communications system. Meanwhile, Belgium's economy profited from the minerals and crops that Belgian-owned companies and plantations were producing in the colony.

Christian missionaries expanded their work in the Belgian Congo. Some of them believed that Congolese society would be more like Europe's if the people became Christians. Some Congolese accepted the Christian faith, but others resisted the missionaries' efforts at conversion. The colonial government supported mission schools, which taught job skills as well as Christian beliefs.

In some places, new sects arose that combined Christian teachings with African religious ideas. Some of these sects openly opposed Europe's influence on African culture. One of the most important of the opposition movements in the Belgian Congo was Kimbanguism, named after its founder, Simon Kimbangu, a popular healer of the time. His views challenged the authority of the Europeans and of the European-run missions. Because this sect's demonstrations in the southern

Belgian Congo disrupted industry, Belgian officials imprisoned Kimbangu in 1921.

WORKING CONDITIONS

By the 1920s, most Congolese workers were employed in mining copper, in gathering rubber, and in harvesting crops for export. But diseases and harsh labor practices had sharply decreased the number of laborers. Colonial officials started a public-health program to ensure that there would be enough healthy workers to fill the mining and farming jobs.

In the mid-1920s, some of the large mining companies decided they needed permanent labor forces. The companies improved working conditions, raised wages, and made contracts with Congolese men to work for three years or longer.

The colony's overall economy faltered during the worldwide depression of the 1930s. Companies fired many workers, some of whom moved to urban centers. During the decade, the Belgian government resettled some Congolese families in new farming communities. Up-to-date equipment and modern farming methods allowed these new settlements to increase their production of cash crops.

The Road to Independence

In the 1940s, conflicts in Europe again affected the Belgian Congo. In 1940 Germany invaded and occupied Belgium, which was heavily bombed during World War II (1939-1945). Mines in Katanga (modern Shaba) supplied copper, tin, cobalt, and other minerals to the nations fighting against Germany. Congolese soldiers fought German forces in Libya and Ethiopia on the African continent.

After the war, revenue from the Belgian Congo's exports helped to rebuild Belgium. Despite their contributions to Belgium's recovery, the Congolese had little influence on the colonial government. In fact, strikes at several mining sites showed how deeply dissatisfied many Congolese were with colonial rule.

In the 1940s and 1950s, a small middle class of mission-educated, French-speaking Congolese began to form. Because of their schooling, many of these people felt separated from traditional African institutions. The Belgians called these Congolese *évolués* (meaning "the civilized ones"). Yet évolués were not truly part of the colonial power structure and had little opportunity to participate in running the colony.

The middle-class Congolese gradually realized that the colonial government was ignoring many issues important to colonized peoples in the region. Some évolués formed regional organizations that supported freedom from colonial control for the Belgian Congo.

In 1956, in Leopoldville, a group of évolués headed by Joseph Ileo proposed a long-range program of political reform. A rival association—the Alliance of the Kongo People (ABAKO)—supported Ileo. ABAKO also insisted, however, that the colonial government immediately provide rights of free association, of free speech, and of freedom of the press.

Although Belgian leaders did not grant these rights, the movement for national independence gained strength. Opponents of the colonial government were further encouraged in 1958, when France began to withdraw from its colonies in Africa.

An additional boost to the independence movement came in December 1958, when Patrice Lumumba—who headed the multiethnic National Congolese Movement (MNC)—attended the All-African Peoples' Conference in Ghana, West Africa. Speeches and events at the meeting made Lumumba and other Congolese leaders more determined than ever to achieve freedom for their own country.

Independence and Civil War

At a rally in Leopoldville a few weeks later, Lumumba called for full independence for the Belgian Congo. Within a week of the rally, a confrontation between a Belgian official and a Congolese worker sparked several days of rioting.

Photo by Royal Museum of Central Africa

Born in 1925, Patrice Lumumba worked as a postal official in Kisangani. His commitment to the movement for independence prompted him to go in 1957 to Kinshasa, where he founded the National Congolese Movement—a political party with a strong backing among small ethnic groups. After independence in 1960, Lumumba became the nation's first prime minister.

35

This turmoil, as well as falling prices for mineral exports, persuaded Belgium to give up the colony. A conference in early 1960 set June 30 as the date for independence. In the next few months, more than 100 political parties emerged. None of these parties won a majority in the national elections that were held in May 1960.

The goal of the elections was to form the government for the new Democratic Republic of the Congo. After the elections, however, some groups talked of setting up their own independent regimes. A compromise among the parties was finally reached. Under the agreement, Joseph Kasavubu, the ABAKO leader, became president and Lumumba, the head of the MNC, became prime minister. An elected legislature was to be the main lawmaking body.

Conflict and resentment continued to flare up between some Congolese and the Belgians who remained in the country. Despite its political withdrawal from the new republic, Belgium still had strong ties to the mining companies that operated in Katanga. In addition, officers in the colonial army had always been Belgian, and without them the new republic's army was poorly led.

Less than a week after independence, Congolese soldiers mutinied, terrorizing Belgian residents. The soldiers demanded higher pay and better opportunities for promotion. To safeguard its people and economic interests, Belgium evacuated Europeans and sent in paratroopers. Fearful of Belgian occupation, Prime Minister Lumumba asked for peacekeeping troops and administrative assistance from the United Nations (UN), an international organization that the country had joined in 1960.

At the same time, conflict was brewing in the copper-rich southern region of Katanga. On July 11, its self-proclaimed president, Moise-Kapenda Tshombe, withdrew the region from the Congo republic.

Photo by Globe Photos, Inc.

Mobutu Sese Seko took over the government in 1965 and quickly eliminated all opposition to his rule. He called huge rallies and used posters to create an image of large-scale public support. In this poster, rays of the sun beam from God to Mobutu, who is surrounded by adoring Zairean citizens.

When the neighboring region of West Kasai followed, civil war broke out.

Further political unrest occurred two months later, when President Kasavubu decided to get rid of his rival, Lumumba. He ordered the army, which was under the control of Colonel Joseph-Désiré Mobutu, to arrest the prime minister. Eventually, Lumumba was sent to Katanga, where Tshombe ordered his execution in January 1961.

Turmoil followed the death of Lumumba. The regions of East Kasai and Kivu asserted their independence, and the civil war continued. Tshombe rejected UN plans for peace throughout 1962, but other groups in Africa and on other continents forced him to restore Katanga to the Congo republic. After UN troops withdrew in mid-1963, Tshombe went into exile.

The Mobutu Regime

Although Katanga was quiet, civil war still raged in West Kasai, East Kasai, and Kivu. Kasavubu felt he needed a strong person to settle the conflict and invited Tshombe to return and serve as prime minister. With Kasavubu's backing, Tshombe used Belgian paratroopers and foreign soldiers to subdue the rebels—an action that made him increasingly powerful. Seeing Tshombe as a rival, Kasavubu fired him.

The divided legislature would not accept Kasavubu's choice for a successor to Tshombe. Moreover, the regional rivalries among political parties made it nearly impossible for the national government to function, and it soon became deadlocked. In late 1965, Colonel Mobutu ousted Kasavubu in a nonviolent takeover.

Mobutu established his control throughout the country. He nationalized (switched from private to state ownership) the huge Belgian company that controlled the Congo republic's copper production. To eliminate challenges to his power, he exiled Tshombe. Mobutu further weakened the opposition by pitting ethnic groups against one another.

Artwork by Laura Westlund

First flown in 1971, the Zairean flag carries the colors yellow, green, and red, which many African nations use on their emblems. The raised arm with a torch is the symbol of the Popular Movement of the Revolution—Mobutu's political party.

In elections held in November 1970, Mobutu—the only candidate—won a seven-year term as president. He got rid of the office of prime minister and made his party, the Popular Movement of the Revolution (MPR), the country's sole legal political party.

In the 1970s, to strengthen the nation's pride in its African heritage, Mobutu began a program of "Zaireanization." It included steps to lessen European influence on Zaire's society and economy. On October 27, 1971, for example, Mobutu changed the Congo's name to the Republic of Zaire (from the Bantu word *nzari*, meaning "river"). He even altered his own name from Joseph-Désiré Mobutu to Mobutu Sese Seko and insisted that other citizens adopt purely African names. The European names of most of the country's cities, towns, and regions also changed.

To diminish European influence on the economy and to emphasize his power, the president nationalized more industries and many farms. The government borrowed large amounts of foreign money to run the new state-owned enterprises. But mismanagement caused production to fall, and in late 1974 the government returned portions of the farms and companies to private ownership. At the same time, the price of copper—the nation's principal export—dropped sharply, making it difficult for the government to pay its foreign debt.

Recent Events

As Zaire struggled economically in the mid-1970s, it was also weakened by its political involvement in neighboring Angola's civil war. The conflict forced the

Conflicts in the 1960s and 1970s forced many Zaireans to find safety in refugee camps. These refugees line up to collect food rations in the Shaba region.

Leading members of the Sacred Union—an anti-Mobutu alliance—gathered in Kinshasa in 1991. Ferdinand Ngomo Ngabu *(left front)* heads the Federalist Christian Democrats. Joseph Ileo *(center front),* leader of the Social and Christian Democratic party, participated in efforts to win Zaire's independence from Belgium in the 1950s. Etienne Tshisekedi *(right front)* directs the Union for Democracy and Social Progress.

closing of Angola's Benguela Railroad, which was Zaire's main transportation route for copper shipments from Shaba to the Atlantic coast. Mobutu, who supported the losing faction in the Angolan civil war, failed to realize his goal of becoming a powerful influence among African countries.

Meanwhile, in 1977 and 1978, Katangan rebels living in Angola attacked Shaba and later occupied the town of Kolwezi. Airplanes dropped Zairean, Moroccan, French, and Belgian paratroopers, who fought to regain control of the town. Hundreds of people were killed in several days of fighting. After international forces recaptured Kolwezi, an all-African force was established to keep peace in the region.

Zaire's problems continued throughout the 1980s. Foreign minister Karl I Bond Nguza—who had openly accused Mobutu's government of corruption—resigned and went into exile. When some members of Zaire's parliament attempted to form their own party in 1982, they were arrested and convicted of treason.

During this time, the annual inflation rate reached 100 percent. To reduce it, the government decreased imports but also cut some health services, educational programs, and social-welfare benefits. These measures, which hurt the majority of Zaireans, did not affect wealthy citizens, nor did the actions curb the inflation rate. The gap between rich and poor continued to widen in 1984, when Mobutu was elected to a third term as president. He pledged to improve transportation, communications, education, and health services, but the standard of living continued to decline.

In the late 1980s, international banks and European governments charged Mobutu and his administration with corrupt practices. Much of the money loaned to Zaire could not be traced. Furthermore, many lenders believed the funds had ended up in Mobutu's private treasury, which was estimated to be worth $5 billion. The charges caused some lenders, including Belgium and the United States, to withhold more aid until stronger democratic practices are in force.

In 1990, after surviving 25 years of turmoil as Zaire's leader, Mobutu promised to move his country toward a freer political system. He legalized opposition political parties, many of which later called for his resignation. Throughout 1991 Zaire's political stability wavered. Mobutu postponed a national conference that was supposed to lead to a more open government. Riots erupted in Kinshasa, where unpaid soldiers looted stores and destroyed property. French and Belgian residents fled, leaving schools and clinics throughout the country understaffed. Food shortages occurred, followed by a decline in medical supplies.

By early 1992, Mobutu was still trying to maintain his hold on power. Meanwhile, opposition groups continued to press for change in the government. Zaireans, as well as international organizations, await the outcome of what may be the most chaotic period of Zaire's history.

Government

The Zairean constitution adopted in 1974 concentrates authority in the office of the president. The president can declare war, can make treaties, and can impose a state of emergency without the approval of any other governmental body or official. Ac-

In the fall of 1991, Mobutu agreed to rule with the help of a cabinet dominated by opposition leaders. Tshisekedi *(above)*—a long-time rival of Mobutu—became the country's prime minister, but Mobutu fired him from the post in October of that year.

cording to the constitution, a president cannot serve more than two consecutive terms. Mobutu, however, had the law changed to give himself the right to run for president an unlimited number of times. In 1990 the office of prime minister was reinstated. The person appointed to this position runs the nation's day-to-day affairs.

The president names members of the courts, the legislature, and the executive branch. The constitution provides for a unicameral (one-house) legislature. Zaire's judges hear cases at the local and appeals levels. The highest court is the supreme court, which can judge cases from all other courts.

For the purposes of local administration, Zaire is divided into eight regions. The capital city of Kinshasa forms a separate, ninth region. Each region has zones that are run by government-appointed officials. Traditional leaders maintain order in the smallest administrative units, known as collectives.

The coat of arms of Zaire features the head of a leopard snarling over a crossed arrow and spear. Flanking the image are a palm branch and an elephant's ivory tusk. Beneath the emblem are the French words for justice, peace, and labor.

Political turmoil and a slow economy have had a strong impact on Zaire's youngest citizens. Many children, such as these from the Kivu region, lack food, schooling, and health care.

3) The People

Most of Zaire's 37.8 million people are poor and live in rural areas. Although farming supplies only one-fourth of the nation's income, it employs three-fourths of the people. The average annual income per person is low—less than $300. Most Zaireans have a hard time making enough money to feed, clothe, and shelter their families.

Zaire also has a high rate of population growth. At the current rate of increase—3.1 percent—Zaire's population will double in 22 years. More than half of the nation's citizens are younger than 16 years of age, and two-thirds are younger than 25. The high growth rate concerns the Zairean government, but efforts to curb the increase have not been widely successful so far.

Ethnic Groups

More than 200 ethnic groups live in Zaire, giving the nation a rich variety of cultures and languages. Most Zaireans fall into one of four major categories. About 70 percent of the population belong to Bantu-speaking groups. Another 20 percent are of Sudanic background, meaning that their ancestors came from lands north of Zaire, probably from southern Sudan. The Mbuti and other rain-forest dwellers form 7 percent of the population, and 3 percent are members of

Nilotic groups. Nilotic peoples have historic ties to regions near the Nile River. About 50,000 non-Africans, mostly Belgians, also make their homes in Zaire.

Among the major Bantu-speaking groups are the Mongo, the Luba, the Lunda, the Kongo, and the Lulua. The Mongo live throughout the cuvette and in a large area of the Southern Uplands bordered by the Lulonga, Momboyo, and Lualaba rivers. The Luba, who dwell in Kasai and Shaba, tend to be highly independent of the central government. Many Luba are mission educated and hold positions of authority in business and in the civil service of Shaba. The Lunda, a people ethnically related to the Luba, dominate southern Shaba, southwestern Kasai, and the southeastern tip of the Bandundu region.

The Zande and Mangbetu, who are Sudanic peoples, live near the Ubangi and Uele rivers. The lifestyles of the Mbuti

Photo by John Edward Hayashida

Accustomed to the life of the hunter, this Mbuti man searches the Ituri Forest, a thickly wooded area of eastern Zaire, for his daily food.

Courtesy of National Museum of African Art, Eliot Elisofon Archives, Smithsonian Institution

A Zande farm couple hoe the field outside their village in northeastern Zaire.

Every day, Zairean women pound grains or leaves into fine powders that can be used as flour or spices.

Zairean families are often large, with older children caring for the younger ones. In the Kivu region, a girl named Furaha, which means "happiness" in the Kiswahili language, cuddles her baby sister Mapendo, whose name means "love."

have changed little since ancient times. They still hunt and gather food in the rainforests of Zaire. Short in stature, the Mbuti number less than 100,000 and are scattered in regions near the equator. The Mbuti speak éfé, a central Sudanic language.

Nilotic peoples, such as the Alur and the Kakwa, make their homes in the northeastern part of the country. Nilotic groups also live in Uganda, Rwanda, and Burundi.

WAY OF LIFE

Zaireans have strong family, clan, and ethnic ties. Women play an important role in traditional Zairean society, which dominates rural areas. In fact, some Zairean groups trace their kinship through the mother instead of through the father.

Villages are the most common unit of social organization. A small village may consist of about 20 dwellings, while a large village usually has about 100 homes. In these communities, women cultivate crops, collect firewood, and cook, while men hunt and fish. Villagers tend to grow and gather only enough food to feed their families. Older children commonly share the jobs of pounding cassava or dried bananas into flour and watching the younger children while their parents work. Most Zairean families are large and often include grandparents and other family members.

Like other developing countries in Africa, Zaire has a very small middle class. Because the nation's economy is weak and wages are low, most salaried workers, urban professionals, and businesspeople need second jobs to support their families. Many young, educated Zaireans get well-paying government appointments, usually through a close relative or through a political connection. Some appointees use money earned in these positions to invest in their own businesses.

The rapid growth of the nation's cities has created a large number of urban poor people. Most have arrived from rural areas in search of jobs and schooling.

Religion

About 60 percent of Zaireans are members of traditional African religions or of sects that combine Christian and traditional African beliefs. Traditional African religions vary widely but generally are based on the principle of a central life force that controls the behavior of people, objects, and nature. Some religious rituals honor ancestors or celebrate the passage from one stage of life to another. Other rites attempt to influence the forces that govern natural cycles, such as seasonal rainfall or fertility.

Although there are several regional sects that combine Christian and traditional African religious beliefs, Kimbanguism is perhaps the only one of nationwide importance. The sect began in the 1920s and is officially called the Church of Jesus Christ on Earth by the Prophet Simon Kimbangu. Its three million members mainly come from Lower Zaire. A strict biblical sect, Kimbanguism promotes African culture but not the use of magic and sorcery. This church was the first independent African church admitted to the World Council of Churches, which encourages cooperation and goodwill among all Christian sects.

About 30 percent of Zaireans are Christians, and, of that percentage, most are Roman Catholic. In 1972 the government consolidated all Protestant sects into a single organization, the Church of Christ in Zaire. About 10 percent of Zaireans are Muslims and follow the Islamic faith. They are the descendants of Arab and African traders who came to Zaire from eastern Africa.

Education

Since gaining its independence in 1960, Zaire has made considerable progress in

Courtesy of John Vreyens

Broad avenues lead to the domed Roman Catholic cathedral in Bukavu, a city on the shores of Lake Kivu.

After participating in a Christian wedding service, the bride and groom return to their village to enjoy traditional festivities.

Young students wait to enter their schoolrooms in Mabalya, a town near Butembo in eastern Zaire.

establishing new schools. Nevertheless, the nation's educational program has had too little money and too few qualified instructors to succeed completely. About three-fourths of Zairean children go to primary school, and roughly one-fourth attend secondary school. By the early 1990s, roughly half of the population could read and write.

During the colonial period, Catholic missionaries and other religious groups ran most of the primary schools in Zaire. Under the Zaireanization movement of the mid-1970s, the government phased out religious instruction and by 1976 had taken full control of education.

At that time, many schools lacked books and other important supplies, and teachers sometimes went for months without pay. As a result, some instructors left their classes during the day to work at second jobs. To improve the educational situation, the government relaxed its policy toward religious schools in the late 1970s. By the early 1990s, church-run institutions were once again educating most young Zaireans.

One of the government's main goals at the secondary and postsecondary levels is to train Zaireans in key technical and managerial skills. The achievement of this goal would end the country's reliance on foreign experts to run factories and to manage offices. Most of the nation's university graduates receive their degrees from one of the campuses of the National University of Zaire, which are at Kinshasa, Kisangani, Kananga, and Lubumbashi.

Health

Government health services, which are available primarily in cities, are generally of poor quality. The country has 1 physician for every 15,000 people. Only one-fifth of Zairean children are immunized against common diseases, such as measles. At major industrial sites, corporations furnish health care to their workers. Rural areas depend chiefly on church-run missions for medical attention. Life expectancy at birth is 52 years—a low figure among industrialized countries but about average for African nations.

Zaire's infant mortality rate—83 deaths per 1,000 live births—is lower than the average for Africa. One of the leading causes of death among infants and young children is severe malnutrition, a result of the protein-poor Zairean diet. Dysentery (severe diarrhea) and parasites are also major hazards to public health.

Malaria, which mosquitoes spread in equatorial regions, is a serious sickness afflicting many adult Zaireans. Acquired immune deficiency syndrome (AIDS) threatens all Zaireans. As of early 1992, health-care professionals had documented more than 11,000 cases of AIDS in Zaire. The tsetse fly spreads encephalitis (sleeping sickness) to humans and animals in low-lying areas and prevents the raising of cattle in the cuvette.

Zaireans seek modern medical treatment for some of these illnesses, but people also depend on traditional cures from village

Courtesy of John Vreyens

A teacher helps his class through an English lesson. Zaire operates roughly 10,000 elementary schools and has about 4,000 secondary schools. The number of students per teacher is high in many Zairean classrooms.

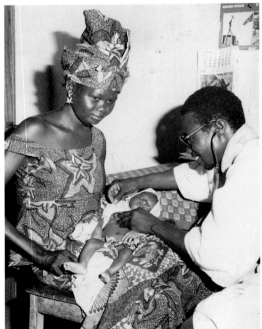

Photo by Bernice K. Condit

At a local clinic, a Zairean infant sleeps through a doctor's examination. Basic health care is hard to find in Zaire, and many children die within the first five years of life.

46

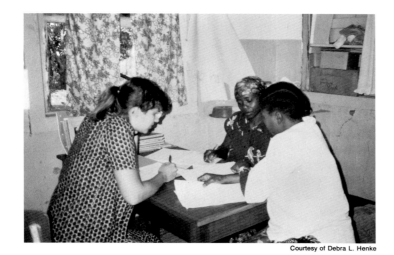

Working with a visiting health-care professional, Zairean women discuss ideas about maintaining a healthful diet. Vegetables and fruits are sometimes scarce, and many families suffer from lack of basic foods.

Courtesy of Debra L. Henke

Signs in Kiswahili advertise veterinary supplies at a store in Bibwe, a village near Goma in the Kivu region.

Courtesy of John Vreyens

healers. These specialists perform surgical procedures and treat wounds and illnesses with medicines made from herbs and other plants. Members of international health organizations have recognized the healers' effectiveness, especially in curing malaria, dysentery, infections, and diseases carried by parasites.

Language and Literature

All educated Zaireans speak French, the nation's official language, which Belgian colonial officials brought to the region. In addition, most Zaireans know one of several Bantu languages, which can be mutually understood by most Bantu-speaking people.

The Zairean government has given four Bantu languages—Lingala, Kiswahili, Kikongo, and Tshiluba—special status as national languages. Containing many French words, Lingala is commonly spoken by soldiers and officers in the Zairean armed forces. It is also used in regions along the Zaire River from Kinshasa to Kisangani. Kiswahili, which has many Arabic words, dominates the Eastern Highlands. People living between Kinshasa and the Atlantic Ocean—the region of the ancient Kongo kingdom—speak Kikongo. Tshiluba, the Luba language, is used in both of the Kasai regions and in some parts of Shaba.

For generations, Bantu-speakers have passed on their wisdom and traditional values through storytelling. In recent decades, efforts have been made to write down the stories and legends of Zaire's many Bantu-speaking groups. During the colonial period, the French-language poet Antoine-Roger Bolamba drew upon such ancient tales for his work *Esanzo, Songs for My Country*.

Independence in 1960 inspired Zairean authors with new themes, which were expressed in political writings and historical accounts. Among writers of fiction, playwrights have probably made the most notable contributions in modern-day Zaire. In the 1970s, Lisembe Elébé produced plays about striking workers, village life, and the career of Simon Kimbangu.

Zairean novelists, such as Dieudonné Mutombo, Mbwil a Mpang Ngal, and Vumbi Yoka Mudimbe, choose topics that range from the history of the independence movement to the demands of urban existence. Most Zairean authors write in French and have their works published in Belgium or France.

The Arts

Zaire has a rich artistic heritage. Craftspeople from many regions of the country carve masks and statues of wood or stone. Regarded as sources of magical power, masks appear in many ceremonies and are usually hidden when not in use. The Yaka people of the Bandundu region are famous for masks that are part of folk-dancing programs. Kuba masks, considered among the finest in Zaire, depict famous leaders of the Kuba kingdom. The Chokwe people create expressive masks and intricate thrones, some of which are modeled after human figures.

Courtesy of National Museum of African Art, Eliot Elisofon Archives, Smithsonian Institution

Courtesy of National Museum of African Art, Eliot Elisofon Archives, Smithsonian Institution

The colorful masks of Zaire vary in style, usage, and meaning, depending on their ethnic origin. Dancers of the Chokwe peoples *(left)* **and of the Kuba peoples** *(right)* **wear masks during their performances.**

The Luba peoples of southeastern Zaire developed strong artistic styles. The female figure is a popular form, and crafters carve it in different poses to serve as the base for common objects. This sculpture of a kneeling woman, for example, is the support for a stool. Scholars have identified the artisan, the Master of Buli, as the producer of many intricate everyday items.

Photo by Royal Museum of Central Africa

The Yaka also produce jewelry and canes carved with the likenesses of their ancestors. The skills of the Mangbetu people in southern Zaire are reflected in the elaborate decorations and paintings on their dwellings. Nationally known artists include the ceramist Mokengo Kwekwe, the painters Lea Kus and Sadi Matamba, and the copper sculptor Ghenge Baruti.

Music enjoys an important place in the traditional communities of Zaire. In the southern savannas, Mangbetu orchestras include wooden gongs, rectangular drums, large iron bells, and ivory horns with leather handles. The beating of drums and the clinking of metal bracelets accompany the dances of the Ngbandi group.

The Mongo perform a ballet called the *bobongo,* in which several groups are on stage at once. The accompanying orchestra uses the *bonkwasa,* a percussion instrument that is made of bamboo stems, and the *longombe,* a large, five-stringed harp mounted on a box.

Lunda dancers perform to the music of the *njimba,* a curved xylophone made with thin wooden slats that are set on gourds of different sizes. Zaire's Intori dancers enjoyed a favored role at the royal courts of the 1400s and 1500s. The Intori now perform in the cities of Rutshuru and Boma.

Photo by Bernice K. Condit

Near Karawa, villagers enjoy the drumbeats produced by two young musicians.

49

Intori dancers have historically represented the royal warriors of the ancient Zairean kingdoms. In modern times, the dancers perform only on special occasions. Here, they take part in the celebrations that accompany the opening of a village community center.

In modern Zaire, jazz bands have had a strong impact on the nation's musical tastes since the 1960s. Congo jazz and *soukouma* (a Lingala word meaning "shake") dominated the early jazz scene. More recently, the fame of the O.K. Jazz Band of Luambo Makiadi, a musician popularly known as Franco, has spread throughout Africa. His rivals include Kabasele and his African Jazz Band and Tabu Ley, who performs as Lord Rochéreau. The number of jazz bands has increased, and villages as well as cities now boast clubs where enthusiasts can hear hit tunes.

Franco *(right)*, a major figure in the modern Zairean music scene, has introduced African jazz to an international audience.

Men dance at a local celebration in Bibanja, near Goma in Kivu.

Food

Many Zaireans grow their own food or purchase it from local markets. Most citizens cannot afford meat and often eat starchy foods, such as cassava, rice, and sorghum. Vegetables, including sweet potatoes and yams, frequently accompany ordinary

Using a wooden mortar and pestle, women pound cassava tubers to make a flour for *ugali,* a pastelike dough dipped in a sauce before eating.

Villagers raise their grain storage bins off the ground to prevent insects and other animals from spoiling the food.

51

meals. Also popular are bananas, which come in several varieties that can be steamed, boiled, or dried. Dried bananas are ground into a popular flour. To season their dishes, Zaireans use palm oil, tiny hot peppers, and fresh ginger.

On special occasions, a Zairean might dine on *moambe*—chicken cooked in fresh palm oil with peanuts, spices, rice, and spinach. *Makobe,* fish prepared in leaves, is also a favorite main course. Cassava is the foundation of another national special-ty known as *chikwangue*. To prepare the dish, cooks pound starchy cassava roots into a powder, which they then make into a paste. After thickening, the paste is boiled and wrapped in banana leaves.

For adults, popular drinks include the nation's many types of beer, as well as palm wine made from the sap of palm trees. Other alcoholic beverages are dis-tilled from cereals, fruits, and roots. Most urban restaurants offer fruit juices and sparkling waters.

All cities and towns have local mar-kets, called *marchés,* where Zaireans can buy fruits, vegetables, and meat.

Photo by Bernice K. Condit

In the town of Kisenge, a basketful of fish is smoked as a means of pres-ervation. Although fishing is not a big money earner for Zaireans, it does introduce needed proteins into the local diet.

Photo by Daniel H. Condit

Photo by Daniel H. Condit

The Inga Dam spans the Zaire River near the lower end of its course to the Atlantic Ocean. Power lines carry hydroelectricity from the dam to industrial sites farther inland at Kinshasa, Kananga, and Shaba.

4) The Economy

Zaire has a wealth of minerals and agricultural resources. To develop its economy, Zaire has received considerable foreign aid, mainly from the World Bank, the International Monetary Fund (IMF), the United States, and Belgium. The Zairean government has used these funds to build energy plants, to improve transportation links, and to undertake other major projects.

These large loans, combined with rising prices for many necessary goods, have burdened Zaire with a huge foreign debt. In the early 1990s, estimates suggested the country owed more than $8 billion to foreign lenders. The World Bank, the IMF, and lending nations have pressed Zaire to reform its economy. But these international pressures have been only partly successful in reducing the debt.

As a result of the country's sagging economy, the standard of living for most Zaireans continued to fall in the early 1990s. In fact, economists list Zaire among the world's poorest nations. The ability of the average urban worker to purchase goods is much less than it was in 1960. Millions of Zaireans do not have enough food, and many go without such basic items as soap, salt, and shoes.

Mining

In terms of its untapped mineral wealth, Zaire is one of the richest nations in the world. The sale of large deposits of copper, cobalt, and diamonds once allowed mining companies to prosper. These same enterprises are now suffering from drops in global market prices or from poor management.

Mining is centered largely in the southeastern and eastern parts of Zaire. Copper is found in a 60-mile-wide belt in Shaba. Zaire is the seventh largest producer of the metal and supplies about 7 percent of the world's total output.

Shaba also has large amounts of cobalt, zinc, and manganese, along with smaller supplies of gold, silver, cadmium, tin, and coal. A state-owned company—known as Gécamines—controls mining operations in the region.

Zaire is one of the world's largest producers of industrial diamonds. East Kasai and West Kasai contain major diamond deposits, which workers from the Miba Company process at Mbuji-Mayi in East Kasai. Sites in Kivu yield tin, tungsten, and gold. The northeastern part of Upper Zaire is also a key source of gold.

An exception to the dominance of metal in the economy is petroleum production, which occurs in western Lower Zaire. An oil refinery near the town of Moanda on the Atlantic Ocean opened in 1968 and now processes 750,000 tons of oil annually. In 1990 Zaire and Uganda agreed to explore for oil in several lakes that lie along their mutual border.

Courtesy of National Museum of African Art, Eliot Elisofon Archives, Smithsonian Institution

Miners at an open-pit tin mine shovel rocks and soil onto a conveyer belt.

At an oil-pumping station near Kinshasa, welders repair the joint of a major pipeline.

Wearing protective hats and clothing, workers at the Miba Company in Mbuji-Mayi walk toward dredging equipment that searches for diamonds in a nearby riverbed.

Agriculture and Fishing

About half of Zaire's land is suitable for farming, but only 2 percent of the nation's farmable territory is under cultivation. Roughly three-fourths of the work force are farmers, most of whom grow just enough to feed their families and have no surplus food to sell. About half of the export crops are raised on large agricultural estates.

Mismanagement and inexperience during Zaireanization—a nationwide effort to put foreign-owned farms and businesses in Zairean hands—seriously hurt agricultural production. In addition, food prices soared when rains and lack of money destroyed the road network, which distributed food throughout the country. Once an exporter of food, Zaire now grows too little to meet the needs of its own citizens.

In some areas of northern Kivu, the rich volcanic soil can yield three crops in a year. On steeply sloped land, such intense farming can result in soil erosion.

Long horns are the trademark of the Ankole breed of cattle, which are raised in eastern Zaire.

In tropical areas, the major crops are bananas, coffee beans, cotton, corn, millet, cassava, palm oil, rice, rubber, and sugarcane. Less important crops include cacao, peanuts, sorghum, tea, tobacco, and vegetables. A mild climate helps farmers on the high plains of the east and south to produce potatoes, leeks, and coffee beans. The cool temperatures and fertile soil of the Eastern Highlands favor the cultivation of cabbages, onions, tomatoes, and strawberries.

To raise cash crops, workers on large farms clear the ground toward the end of the dry season and plant seeds before the first rain. They harvest export crops—such as coffee, tea, and cotton—at the end of the rainy season. In years when the rainy season is very long, farmers can immediately replant after a harvest and get a second crop. The Zairean government

A worker cuts down a large cluster of ripe bananas from a field in northern Zaire.

recently has taken some steps to improve farming techniques and to develop new, more productive strains of seeds.

Because of diseases transmitted to cattle by the tsetse fly, few ranchers raise these animals in Zaire. Most cattle live in the Southern Uplands and in the Eastern Highlands, where the insect cannot survive. On ordinary farms, chickens, pigs, ducks, geese, and goats are common.

Fishing is not a key industry in Zaire, but it provides people with an important source of food. In the early 1990s, annual catches of both freshwater and saltwater

Farmers have cleared this section of tropical rain-forest in East Kasai to plant cassava, a staple food for most Zaireans.

A fishing crew lays out its catch from a day's work in coastal waters.

fish reached about 200,000 tons. Across rushing rivers, some villagers cooperate to set up elaborate nets that catch catfish and mbenga. The lakes in eastern and southern Zaire are sources of freshwater species, such as tilapia. Kisangani is one of the nation's major fishing ports.

Manufacturing and Trade

Manufacturing accounts for about 7 percent of all goods and services produced in Zaire each year—roughly half the percentage attained in 1960. Good supplies of elec-

tricity and adequate transportation links have made Kinshasa and Lubumbashi the main manufacturing centers. Zairean factories turn out processed food, textiles, construction materials, and transportation equipment.

Poor management and shortages of raw materials, such as steel and iron, hamper Zaire's industrial output. In addition, a lack of spare parts prevents most factories from running at full capacity. In recent years, the government has attempted to improve the situation by offering tax breaks to foreign companies that will build and operate manufacturing facilities in Zaire.

Zaire's economy depends largely on the export of minerals, especially copper, cobalt, industrial diamonds, gold, zinc, and tin. More than 80 percent of the country's export revenues come from minerals. Sixty-five percent is from copper alone. Export crops are the second largest earner of foreign income. Coffee beans and palm oil lead the list of these goods, but timber, rubber, cacao, tea, cotton, and sugarcane are also sold abroad.

Until the late 1980s, Belgium was Zaire's most important trading partner. Other European countries—including France, Germany, Britain, and Luxembourg—are now also becoming major partners. These nations together supply 50 to 75 percent of Zaire's imports and purchase 75 to 80 percent of its exports. The United States and Japan began to be important sources of imports and receivers of exports in the early 1990s.

In recent years, one-third of Zaire's expenditures for imports has been for food. The country also imports manufactured goods, mining machinery, transportation equipment, building materials, textiles, chemical products, and oil.

Transportation

The Zaire River and its tributaries are the backbone of Zaire's transportation system, but waterfalls prevent travel on some parts of these rivers. As a result, shippers and travelers depend on roads and railways to bypass rough sections. Matadi is the main port for seagoing vessels, and there are other harbors along navigable portions of the country's main rivers. In eastern Zaire, Lakes Tanganyika, Kivu, Mobutu Sese Seko, and Rutanzige are

Courtesy of Bill Macheel

Modern equipment helps these workers at a sawmill near Kabinda, East Kasai, to cut and trim logs into building materials.

Heavy rains have turned this dirt road into an impassable, slippery rut.

important transportation routes to points along the eastern Zairean border.

Railroads are also vital to the movement of goods and raw materials across the country. Overland links exist where large quantities of minerals or agricultural products must travel to market. Five railway systems connect the navigable rivers to mining and commercial farming areas. The longest railroad network ties southern Shaba to the port of Ilebo on the Kasai River and ultimately to Kinshasa.

In 1960 Zaire had about 80,000 miles of roads, but most were little more than dirt tracks. The government has not maintained the road system, and heavy annual rainfall leaves many routes rutted and impassable. Less than 5,000 miles of roads remain usable by motorized traffic. In 1990 an international lender provided funds to begin improvements of the rural road network.

With so few roads in such a large country, air travel is increasingly important in

Traveling by river is often much easier than going by road in Zaire. Here, four men pole a boat along the Zaire River.

Zaire. Most business travelers save time by flying on Air Zaire, the state-owned national airline. Zaire has many local airfields, as well as large airports at Kinshasa, Lubumbashi, and Kisangani that can handle international flights. The rainforest and the country's national parks also contain many landing strips.

Open-air buses with metal or canvas roofs are the most common mode of public transportation in Zaire's interior. Before setting off, drivers of these vehicles pack them to overflowing with riders and goods. The pirogue—a long, narrow boat pushed with a pole or a paddle—is a common craft for moving passengers and hauling goods on the nation's rivers.

Energy

Zaire has the capacity to produce large amounts of hydroelectricity. The Inga hydroelectric station—the country's most

The equipment of the Inga Dam dwarfs visitors to the huge hydropower station.

Young women in Kivu collect stumps from old tea bushes to use as firewood for cooking. Most Zaireans do not own electrical appliances. As a result, wood and coal are the most common forms of fuel.

ambitious project and the largest hydro-power plant in Africa—was opened in the 1970s on the lower Zaire River, 25 miles upstream from Matadi. A 1,160-mile, high-voltage transmission line—one of the longest in the world—carries power from Inga to Shaba. Smaller hydroelectrical sites on local rivers also serve Shaba.

Mining and other industrial operations consume more than three-quarters of Zaire's total electrical output. Residential use is very limited, since less than 2 percent of the population have access to electricity.

Explorers found petroleum deposits off Zaire's coast in the early 1970s, and drilling began in 1975. By the mid-1980s, oil fields were in production under Zairean partnerships with U.S., Japanese, and Belgian companies. Oil has also been discovered on an island at the mouth of the Zaire River. In addition, after three years of talks, Uganda and Zaire agreed to search for oil in several lakes along their border.

Tourism

Tourism is a new industry in Zaire, but it is slowly gaining importance in the overall economy. Tour operators, travel agencies, and a national tourism department promote the country's wealth of natural beauty and wildlife. Recent spending patterns by visitors to Zaire suggest that the nation could earn more than $20 million a year from tourism.

The Zairean government has established several national parks and reserves. Many of these places are in the Eastern Highlands or in the rain-forest, which shelters thousands of unusual animals and plants. The parks allow visitors to observe mountain gorillas, okapi, white rhinoceroses, elephants, and other creatures in the wild.

The local cultures of Zaire's many ethnic groups also attract visitors. Some tours take travelers through Mbuti villages, where the hunting and gathering lifestyle

Courtesy of John Vreyens

Zaire's tourism industry is dependent on the health and growth of the nation's wildlife populations, which draw vacationers from around the world. Here, a female mountain gorilla carries her baby on her back through the dense vegetation in Kahuzi-Biega National Park.

Courtesy of National Museum of African Art,
Eliot Elisofon Archives, Smithsonian Institution

The masks of the Kuba peoples are known for their expressive representations of famous Kuba kings.

Economic problems and political instability cloud the future of Zaireans of all ages. The turmoil of the early 1990s lowered the standard of living for ordinary citizens, curbed growth in the number of jobs, and reduced the availability of food and medicines.

of the earliest Zaireans is still followed. Zairean carvings are prized for their quality and historical significance. Zairean music, including jazz and traditional dancing, draw international enthusiasts.

The Future

In 1960, when Zaire became independent, its many ethnic groups had no strong sense of nationhood, despite their common effort to gain freedom from Belgium. Mobutu's long regime held the nation together in its early troubled times. His recent policies are returning the country to chaos.

Corruption charges against Mobutu and against politicians in his administration have caused many nations, including Belgium, to withhold their financial support. Violent protests and rioting have disrupted trade and have frightened away investors and non-Zairean professionals.

The standard of living for most Zaireans is continuing to decline.

Because of its extensive natural resources, Zaire has the potential to become one of the African continent's most prosperous nations. The country's success hinges partly on making political reforms and on putting a fair, efficient government in place.

By early 1992, Zaire's economic and political progress had nearly stopped. Mobutu's weak efforts to open up his government showed his unwillingness to share power with opposition groups. The loss of international aid to feed the nation's citizens and to develop the economy hit many Zaireans hard. Food was more scarce than ever, and jobs were difficult to find. Although many countries have distanced themselves from Mobutu, Zaire faces an uncertain future with or without the aging president.

Index